Country Style Appliques for Every Day

Dress up your kitchen with these country designs. An apple basket trims a potholder and quilt designs decorate the tote bag. * Vegetables add pizzazz to a white butcher apron. Make your own reversible apron * with checkerboard trim and a branch of cherry hearts.

Here are the twins, Emily and Peter Croswell, ready for supper in their terrycloth towel bibs. * Appliques of country "critters" are used for trim. Make these practical and colorful bibs with instructions in this book.

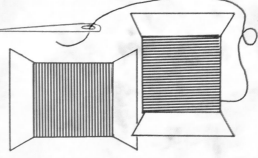

Clothing is no longer plain with the addition of country appliques. Geese and a wagon on button wheels create a "designer sweatshirt." Three snowmen add instant personality to a sweatshirt vest. An appliqued spool necklace * with ribbons dresses up an ordinary knit top. An aqua t-shirt becomes a "class act" with the addition of a quilting design in orange and dark green.

* Make these items with instructions from this book.

Soft peach tones add subtle shades to the country appliques featured here. A fringed collar * with a tulip basket adds a special touch to a plain shirt. An embroidery hoop frames a circle of tulips * and also becomes part of the applique design on the small tote bag. * The monogrammed ultrasuede checkbook cover * features a pen holder. Stationery * and note cards can also be trimmed with applique designs.

In the bedroom, country designs give personality to ordinary objects. Blue geese are stitched onto "hopscotch" fabric and framed with old-fashioned cross-bars. The pillowcases * feature two floral designs. Three country sisters trim a decorator pillow and three "counted" sheep add a whimsical touch to a bright pink heating pad cover. *

* Make these items with instructions from this book.

Country Style Appliques

Applique Designs and Instructions for Sewing Projects

by Mary Mulari

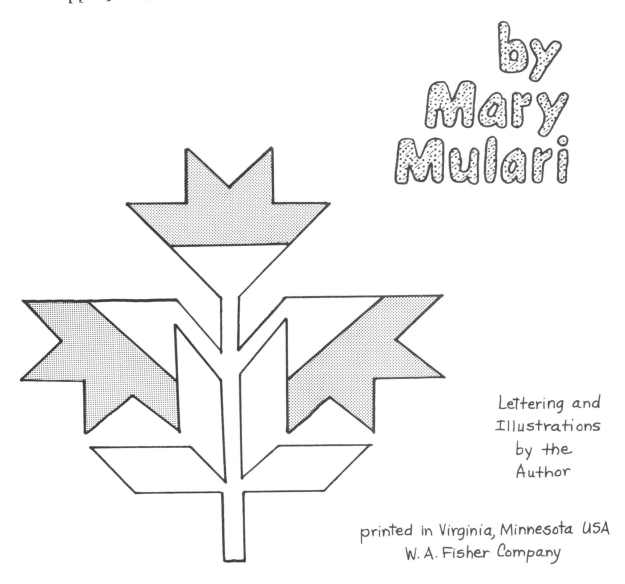

Lettering and
Illustrations
by the
Author

printed in Virginia, Minnesota USA
W. A. Fisher Company

In appreciation to:

Margaret Croswell
Nancy Harp
Rhonda Zuponcic

Photography by G.W. Tucker Photographic Studio, Virginia, Minnesota

Photo of Emily and Peter Croswell by Margaret Croswell.

ISBN 0-9613569-5-2

Third Printing: January 1989

Country Angel

Hair and eyes may be added with dots of fabric paint, small snaps, satin-stitched circles or French Knots.

Optional apron is indicated by the dotted line.

Table of Contents

This book is dedicated
to honor the memories of

Sandra Kangas Adams
Babs Durning
Chuck Soukup

Also by Mary Mulari:

Designer Sweatshirts
Applique Design Collection
MORE Designer Sweatshirts

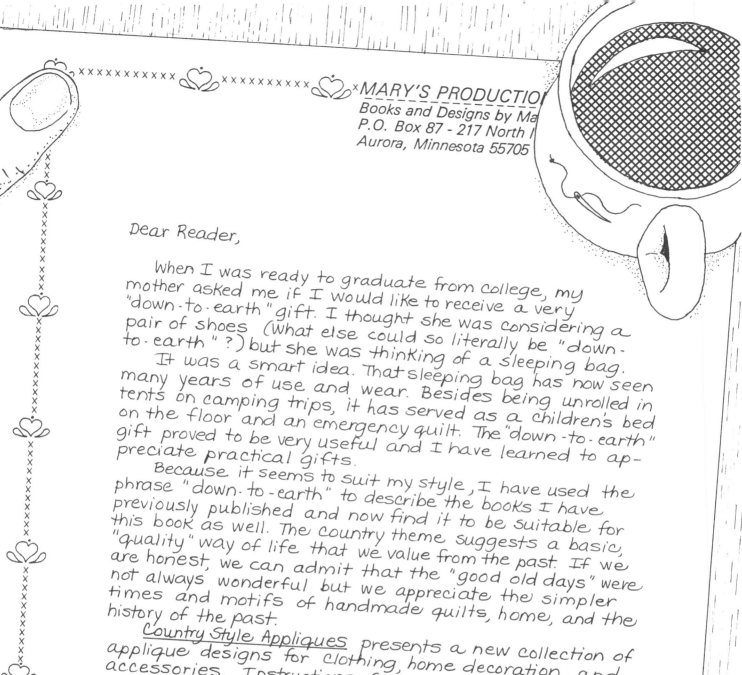

MARY'S PRODUCTIO[...]
Books and Designs by Ma[...]
P.O. Box 87 - 217 North [...]
Aurora, Minnesota 55705

Dear Reader,

When I was ready to graduate from college, my mother asked me if I would like to receive a very "down-to-earth" gift. I thought she was considering a pair of shoes (what else could so literally be "down-to-earth"?) but she was thinking of a sleeping bag.

It was a smart idea. That sleeping bag has now seen many years of use and wear. Besides being unrolled in tents on camping trips, it has served as a children's bed on the floor and an emergency quilt. The "down-to-earth" gift proved to be very useful and I have learned to appreciate practical gifts.

Because it seems to suit my style, I have used the phrase "down-to-earth" to describe the books I have previously published and now find it to be suitable for this book as well. The country theme suggests a basic, "quality" way of life that we value from the past. If we are honest, we can admit that the "good old days" were not always wonderful but we appreciate the simpler times and motifs of handmade quilts, home, and the history of the past.

Country Style Appliques presents a new collection of applique designs for clothing, home decoration, and accessories. Instructions for related sewing projects are also included. It is my hope that you will find this book to be a source of new ideas and brainstorms that will lead to many hours of enjoyable sewing.

Sincerely,

Mary Mulari

Comments about Machine Applique

This book is designed as a resource for country applique patterns and projects to sew rather than a primer in beginning applique. If you have been enjoying machine applique already, you may have your own favorite techniques. If you are a beginner, you will need to read and learn about new methods and materials which will make this kind of sewing easier and also, you'll need to practice.

More detailed instructions for applique can be found in my books *designer sweatshirts* and *MORE designer sweatshirts*. Included here is a list of materials and some suggestions which may be helpful to you.

Materials for machine applique:

- new sewing machine needle
- pins
- iron

- good quality fabrics for applique shapes, matching thread
- Stitch N Tear Pellon or tearaway stabilizer
- typing (or other see-through) paper for tracing
- Wonder-Under™ or Teflon® pressing sheet and Stitch Witchery

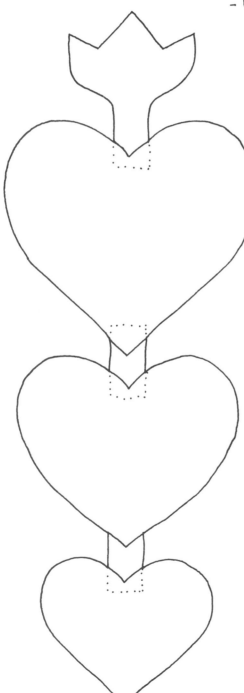

To begin . . .

1. Trace your applique design onto paper which you can cut apart. If the design has many pieces, trace each piece separately. If you want to "flip" a design to face in the opposite direction, reverse the paper shapes after cutting.

 ← tracing paper with all parts of design on this page

2. Cut blocks of fabric slightly larger than the design shapes. Using either Wonder-Under™ or a Teflon® pressing sheet with Stitch Witchery, make the wrong side of the fabric fusible by following the directions for the product you are using. Then cut the design shape from the treated fabric.

3. For pieces to be joined together, plan that one piece will overlap the other. For example, sections of the tulip stem connecting the hearts on this page are cut longer so hearts can overlap the stem pieces. Try to avoid placing other color fabrics under white design shapes to avoid "shadowing" through the white.

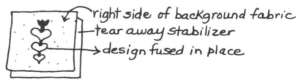

right side of background fabric

tear away stabilizer

design fused in place

4. Position design shapes on garment or fabric background. Fuse in place with the iron. Pin a piece of tearaway stabilizer larger than the design area directly beneath it on the wrong side of the background fabric.

5. Use the machine applique stitch with slightly loosened top tension. Change top thread to match applique fabrics; bobbin thread can remain the same for all applique stitching.

Stop machine and pivot fabric at locations indicated by dots. This will create a smooth continuous stitching line.

Stitch around the shapes, pull threads to the back and knot them. Tear away the stabilizer. *Enjoy!*

Heating Pad Cover with "Counting" Sheep

How about a new cover for your heating pad or hot water bottle? It may be an idea you've never considered, but it's likely that anyone's heating pad could use a new cover with an applique. Think about this for a gift idea, too.

Measure the heating pad and cut 2 pieces of fabric 2" wider and 4" longer than the measurements. (mine measures 12" wide x 14" long so I cut my fabric pieces 14" W. x 18" L.) Heavy weight flannel, sweatshirt fleece or other soft fabrics would be good choices for a new cover. Add appliques before assembling.

With right sides together, stitch or serge around the sides & bottom of the cover fabrics. This will create a small "pillowcase."

wrong side of fabric

Turn back the raw edge at the top of the case to form a hem about 1" wide and stitch hem in place around the cover.

Velcro

To hold the heating pad inside the new cover, add Velcro to the top hem inside the cover. Make sure you place the Velcro so the electric cord has a clear opening from the cover. One 2" piece of Velcro centered across the hem of the cover will usually work well.

wrong side of fabric

Think warm thoughts as you snuggle with your new "designer" heating pad. Then take it to the kitchen next time you need a warm place to raise yeast dough. (maybe I should write a cookbook next . . .)

length
width

white
black
black
black
black
black

black
white
black
black

Dashed lines indicate stitching lines for added detail and shape

black
white
black
black

black
black

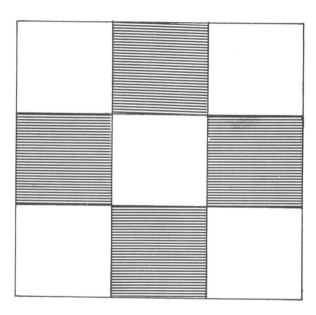

Quilting Squares

These quilting patterns are designed as 3" squares to mix and match. Consider the solid dark colors used by the Amish for their quilts.

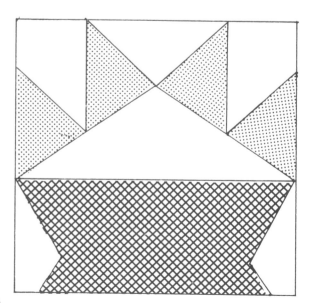

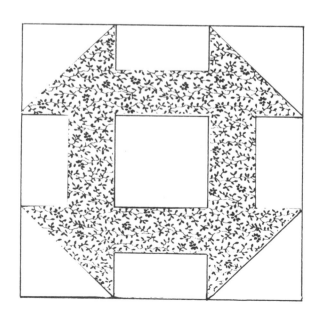

Tote Bags to Make

When you would like to carry your equipment in a bag more durable and attractive than a plastic bag from a store, make your own tote bag and add an applique.

Make your bag as large or small as you'd like. Dimensions given here are for an average size bag 12" x 12".

Materials needed: 1 yd. sturdy fabric (such as poplin) with thread to match
1 yd. for lining (optional)
1 yd. webbing or strapping for handles — or use bag fabric.

Layout for cutting fabric

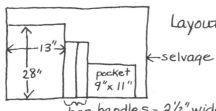

For lining, cut 1 piece of lining fabric 13" x 28"
option — a pocket in the lining

bag handles - 2½" wide x 15-18" long

Let's begin by sewing the pocket for the outside of the bag. Iron back ½" on the sides and bottom edges of the pocket fabric. Iron back the top edge twice so the raw edge is enclosed. Stitch across the top to attach this edge. Decorate the right side of the pocket with an applique.

Fold tote bag body in half and position the pocket about 3" above the foldline and centered on the bag fabric. Stitch around the pocket's sides and bottom to attach it to the tote bag.

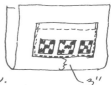

To construct the bag, we'll begin by folding the bag fabric in half with right sides together. Sew or serge up each side. If lining the bag, sew lining fabric sides in the same way. Turn lining right side out and slip over the wrong side of the tote bag fabric.

To form a rectangular bottom to the bag, keep the lining side out and fold the bottom corner to a "v" shape so the side seamline is directly over the center bottom fold of the bag. Stitch across the "v" about 1½" above the point. Sew the same seam on the other corner of the bag.

Bag Handles: Cut the webbing or strapping material into 2 pieces (15-18" is a good length for each handle) or sew fabric strips into handles. Fold strips in half lengthwise. Stitch the long edges together. Turn right side out.

wrong side

Set the handles aside while you complete the top edge of the bag. Line up the top raw edges of the lining and outer bag fabrics. Turn back the raw edges toward the lining side about ½" and press down. Turn the bag right side out.

Pin the ends of each bag handle to the top edge of the bag, placing the ends about 3" from the bags side seams.

Secure handle ends to bag by stitching a 1" square with reinforcement stitching through the middle, as shown in the diagram. Attach all 4 handle ends in this manner.

Now fold the top edge of the bag down and inside about 1½". Pin around the fold to hold it in place while you stitch from the outer side of the bag so the stitching will be even and smooth. Make sure the sewing machine needle is the correct size to handle fabric thicknesses.

If you have lots to carry, make LARGE tote bags. You can carry more in one trip. Remember: it takes 2 hands to carry one box.

Here's Mary arriving to teach "Designer Sweatshirts" classes with 2 of her 3 large tote bags.

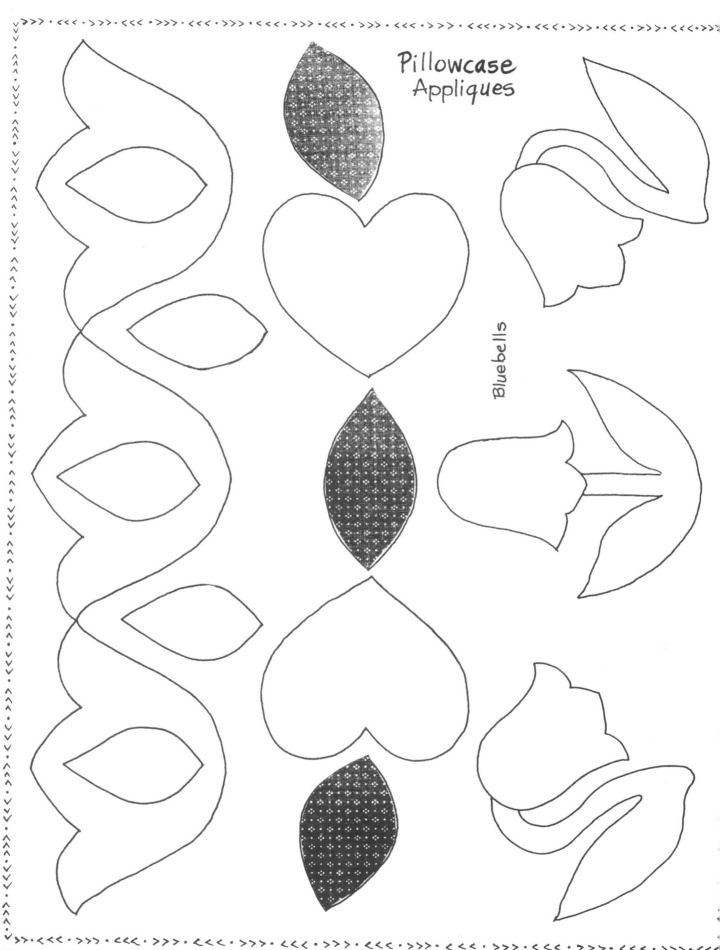

Pillowcase
Appliques

Bluebells

12

Pillowcase Appliques

Pillowcases with country appliques are sure to be appreciated by the home decorator who has chosen a country motif. You can use purchased pillowcases or sew your own for this project.

Measure a ready-made pillowcase or use the yardage estimates given here:

	Finished Size	45" yardage for a pair
Standard	20" x 30"	2 yards
Queen size	20" x 34"	2 1/4 yards
King size	20" x 40"	2 1/2 yards

After sewing across the bottom and up the side of the case, you will be pressing and stitching the top hem. A usual measurement for a pillowcase hem is 4" wide but you may wish to adjust this according to the applique you have chosen.

Because of the large opening, it is easy to applique on the pillowcase after it is completely sewed.

Besides using the designs on these pages, you may want to create some special pillowcases for children. Personalize the cases with a name, initials, or the design of a favorite sport or hobby. For pillows that are toted from room to room or used on a sofa, a dark color might be appreciated by the laundry person.

For a truly creative idea, use a motif or part of a motif, from the bedroom's wallpaper for the applique design on pillowcases.

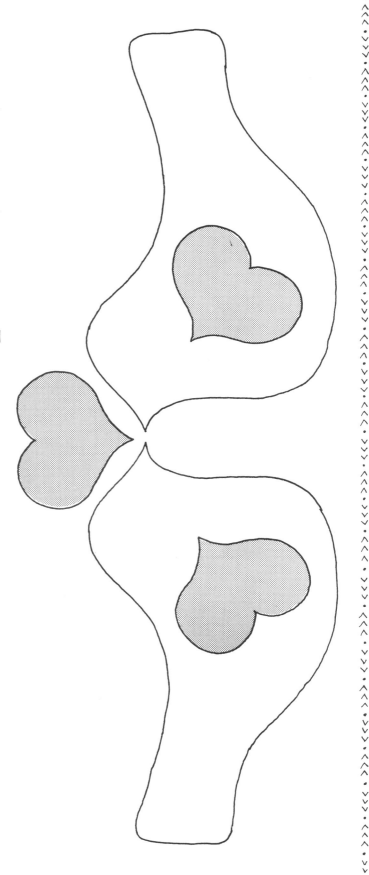

Designs for Baby

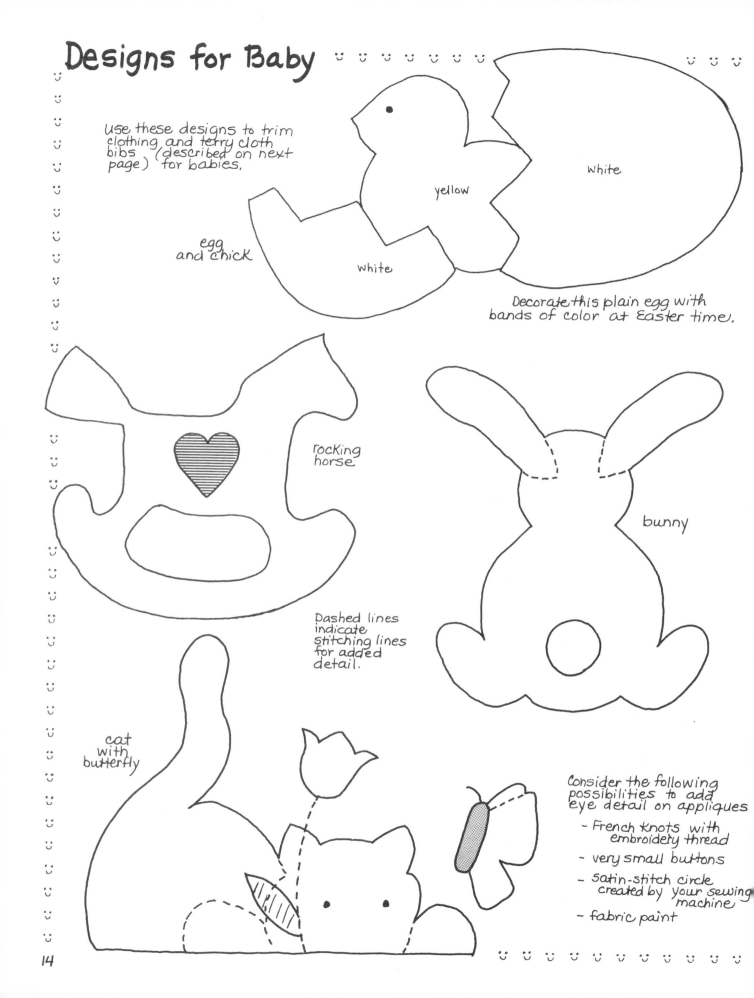

Use these designs to trim clothing and terry cloth bibs (described on next page) for babies.

egg and chick

yellow

white

White

Decorate this plain egg with bands of color at Easter time.

rocking horse

bunny

Dashed lines indicate stitching lines for added detail.

cat with butterfly

Consider the following possibilities to add eye detail on appliques

- French knots with embroidery thread
- very small buttons
- satin-stitch circle created by your sewing machine
- fabric paint

Baby Bibs from Guest Towels

Make a bib for Baby from a terrycloth guest towel and knit ribbing. This bib will stay on (no ties to pull open) and is easy to launder.

Supplies needed:

    one guest towel or:
      - handtowel for an older child or
      - 11" x 16" piece of terrycloth

    one piece of ribbing 11" wide x
      3" long

Trace the neckhole pattern on this page. Fold the towel in half vertically. Place the neckhole pattern about 3" from one end of the towel and on the fold. Pin pattern in place and cut neckhole from towel.

Serge or sew the 2 narrow ends of the ribbing together to form a tube. Bring the cut raw edges of the tube together by folding the tube in half with wrong sides inside.

Divide both the ribbing tube and the towel's neckhole into quarters by folding and marking with pins or a washable marking pen.

wrong side of towel

raw edge of towel and ribbing

Pin the ribbing into the neckhole by matching the quarter marks. Place the seamline of the ribbing at the center back of the neckhole. Stretch the ribbing to fit into the neckline. Add more pins in each section. Serge or sew the ribbing to the towel. A stretch stitch with an overcast edging would be good to use if you have this stitch on your sewing machine.

Now you're ready to applique a design for Baby.

Baby Bib
Neckhole
Pattern

Place this line on lengthwise fold on towel →

P.S. This is a great project for beginning applique.

paperdolls with scissors

Food for A Country Kitchen

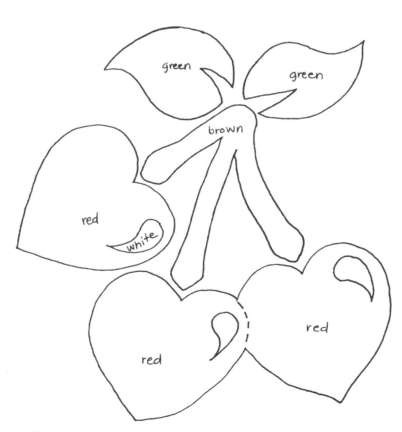

green

green

orange

dark green

medium green

red

dark green

purple

carrots, broccoli and eggplant

green

green

brown

red

white

red

red

red

To create the comma-shaped reflections on these cherries, use a satin stitch and taper it from wide to very narrow. Rayon machine embroidery thread gives a shiny look – I recommend it.

Checkerboard

To make pieced checkerboard like the band on the blue apron on pg. 1, we can use the techniques of strip patchwork.

For a standard red and white checkerboard, cut 2 strips of fabric, one of each color. They must be the same width. (For the apron pictured, I cut two – 1" wide strips about 20" long. Using 1/4" seam allowances, sew the 2 strips together. Press seam allowance toward red strip.

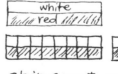

Divide the new strip of fabric into equal portions (I used 1" by drawing lines with a washable marker. Then cut the strip apart on the lines you drew.

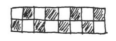

Sew the small pieces together, alternating the colors to build a checkerboard look.

A checkered border adds a country look to aprons, towels, or whatever you have.

Butcher Aprons

For anyone who works in the kitchen, a butcher apron is very useful and practical. Besides, the upper bib section offers a great place for an applique. For ready-made aprons, check a department store's housewares area or a restaurant supply store. These aprons are inexpensive and can be decorated quickly — a good bazaar project.

If you make your own butcher apron, I suggest that you make it reversible. Butcher apron patterns are available from any major pattern company or you can use this grid pattern to make your own. (I know... these aren't my favorite things either, but it is a way to give you a pattern.) Trace the pattern onto tissue or freezer paper.

Also cut these patterns:

    Waist tie - 2" x 29"
    neck strap - 2" x 12"
    pocket - 9" x 9"
    (optional - or vary size)

Each square = 2"

Two yards of 45" fabric are needed for the reversible apron. You can make both sides of the same fabric or use 2 co-ordinating fabrics - buy 1 yard of each. (We'll call them fabric A & B.)

Place both yard pieces of fabric one on top of the other with folds and selvages matching.

Layout:

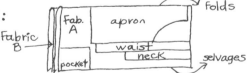

Fabric B
Fab. A
apron
folds
waist
neck
pocket
selvages

You will be cutting 4 layers of fabric at once, cutting 2 apron shapes, 4 waist ties and 4 neck straps. Cut as many pockets as you want for each apron front.

Sewing the Apron:

Sew neck straps and waist ties by placing 1 fabric A piece over 1 fabric B piece, right sides inside. Sew around the sides and one end, using a 1/4" seam allowance. Trim corners and turn strips inside out.

Wrong side

Sew the pockets onto both apron fronts. Add appliques to apron now.

Position all neckbands and waist ties in their correct locations on Apron A. Make sure the A side is facing down. Pin ties into place. Then position Apron B right side down over Apron A and all the ties.

Fabric B
right side - Fabric A

Wrong side - Fabric B

Pin the 2 apron bodies together, making sure the ends of the ties are not in the seamline. (I call this an apron sandwich.) Use 1/4" seam allowance and sew around, leaving a 3" opening on one side. Trim corners and clip seams. Press. Pull the right side out through the opening. Hand stitch opening or fuse shut with Stitch Witchery.

Add Velcro strips about 2" long to the ends of the neck straps. This makes an adjustable neckstrap — very handy if you don't want to ruin your hairdo.

These aprons make wonderful down-to-earth gifts for men, women, and children.

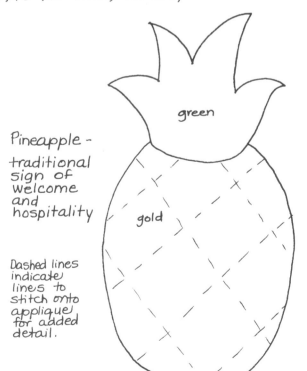

Pineapple - traditional sign of welcome and hospitality

green

gold

Dashed lines indicate lines to stitch onto applique for added detail.

Favorite Flowers

dogwood
add center details
with French knots or
fabric paint

Lavender

Lavender

violets

stitch stems with
green thread

Flowers have proven to be favorite
applique choices for many years.
Select one of these for a special
tote bag, sweatshirt or even a
potholder.

dark
green

Tulip Circle

Eight tulips of this size and positioned in this way will form a circle with an 8" diameter.

See the tulip circle on page 2. The frame is a 10" embroidery hoop.

Something to consider:

A circle of tulips around the neckline of a plain shirt or sweatshirt.

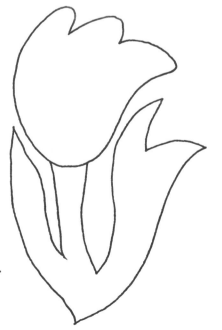

Eight tulips of this size will form a circle with a 10" diameter.

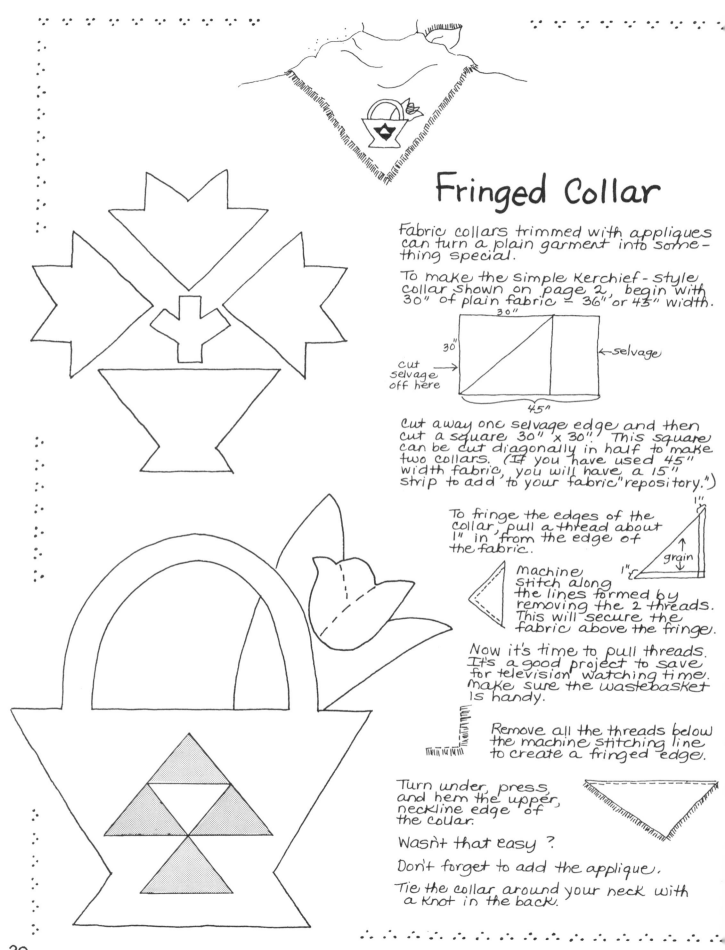

Fringed Collar

Fabric collars trimmed with appliques can turn a plain garment into something special.

To make the simple kerchief-style collar shown on page 2, begin with 30" of plain fabric — 36" or 45" width.

Cut away one selvage edge and then cut a square 30" x 30". This square can be cut diagonally in half to make two collars. (If you have used 45" width fabric, you will have a 15" strip to add to your fabric "repository.")

To fringe the edges of the collar, pull a thread about 1" in from the edge of the fabric.

Machine stitch along the lines formed by removing the 2 threads. This will secure the fabric above the fringe.

Now it's time to pull threads. It's a good project to save for television watching time. Make sure the wastebasket is handy.

Remove all the threads below the machine stitching line to create a fringed edge.

Turn under, press, and hem the upper, neckline edge of the collar.

Wasn't that easy?

Don't forget to add the applique.

Tie the collar around your neck with a knot in the back.

green

←brown

green

red   white

red

Baskets
and
Buckets

This apple basket is featured on a potholder on page 1.

Stitch the handle of this bucket with a satin stitch.

Try these designs in Ultrasuede®

Hearts

These hearts may be cut all in one from the same fabric or cut individually, as shown on the book's back cover.

This patchwork heart is made with 3 different fabrics. (see the front cover) I added a decorative machine stitch between the sections to imitate the look of a crazy quilt.

Hearts for Stitchin'

← add real ribbons and bows to the ends of the string of hearts

Soft pastel colors or remnants of old quilt fabrics would give a subtle and classy look to this string of hearts.

This country-style house
can be found on
the cover of this book.

Town and . . .

No matter where you live now, there may
be a special small town or farm you
remember from the past. It may be
the place you associate with country
motifs and a carefree, comfortable
lifestyle. maybe it's like Lake Wobegon,
Minnesota, the "little town that time
forgot that the decades cannot improve."

Stitch your own village, combining these homes
and buildings. If it's appropriate for your
personalized village, stitch some pine trees
in various shades of dark green behind the
buildings.

school   church

Country

Farm Scene

Add a tractor to your appliquéd farm. (I won't suggest a color to use for the tractor—you can select the color of your favorite brand.)

black

In city and country, birds are welcome visitors and residents.

red

white

gray

brown

Personalize this **mailbox** with a name or initials.

Country Folks

Build a little family group with these children and their trusty teddy bear.

Dashed lines indicate stitching lines to add details.

To make this sunbonnet pair into Amish folks, use solid dark colors such as black, royal blue, and purple.

Add eyes
with paint
or embroidery
by hand.

These 3 sisters decorate a pillow on page 2.

Create their hair
with French knots,
small snaps, or
by stitching
circles of the
satin stitch
at your sewing
machine.

Tiny snaps
sewed around
heads make
interesting
hair. Use
black snaps.

Winter and Christmas

Stitch the snowmen and women's arms with black or brown thread. You may want to use a wider applique stitch also.

yellow

red

green

Sew a grouping of poinsettias to decorate a Christmas apron.

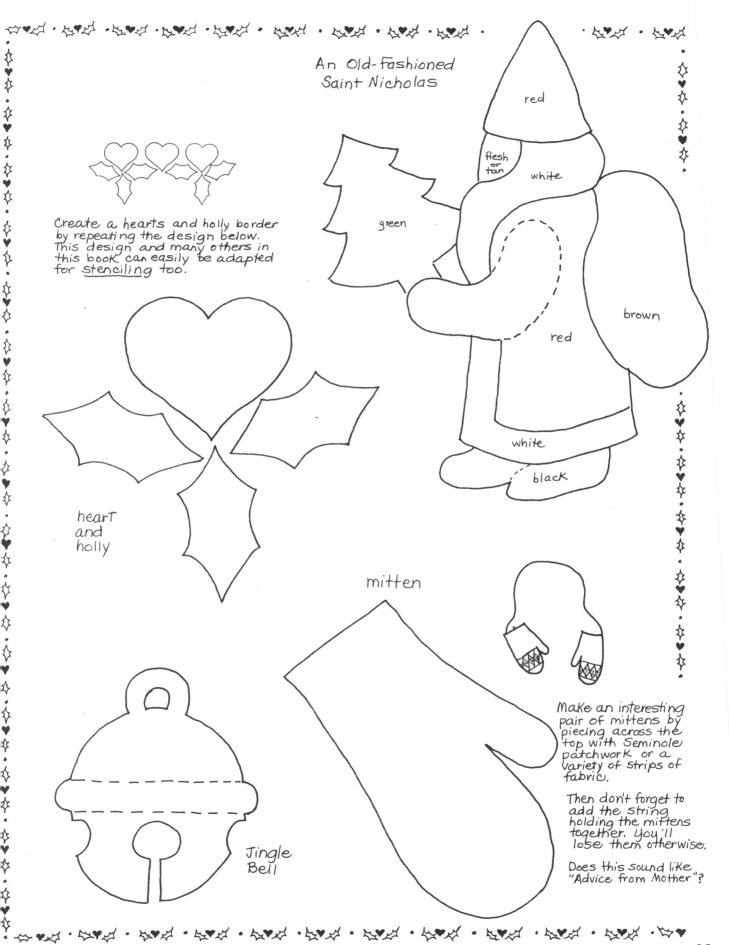

An Old-Fashioned
Saint Nicholas

red

flesh
or
tan

white

green

brown

red

white

black

Create a hearts and holly border
by repeating the design below.
This design and many others in
this book can easily be adapted
for stenciling too.

heart
and
holly

mitten

Make an interesting
pair of mittens by
piecing across the
top with Seminole
patchwork or a
variety of strips of
fabric.

Then don't forget to
add the string
holding the mittens
together. You'll
lose them otherwise.

Does this sound like
"Advice from Mother"?

Jingle
Bell

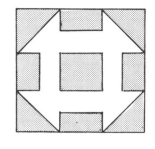

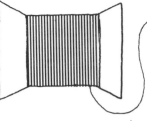

Draw thread from the spool as a border around an envelope or sheet of stationery

Your Own Style Stationery

Express your love of country motifs in your correspondence. It's easy and fun to decorate plain stationery with simple, small designs.

Purchase plain colored notecards or stationery of good quality. You will also need Wonder-Under ™, the fusible backed paper from the fabric or craft store.

Select a design and trace it on the paper side of the Wonder-Under ™. Following the instructions, fuse the Wonder-Under ™ to the back side of a piece of fabric. Tiny print calicoes or solid colors are best for this project. Cut out the design shapes, peel off the paper backing, and fuse the designs onto the stationery and envelope flaps. Your iron should be set on a non-steam setting. Add extra details with a fine line marking pen.

This is a great project for those who like detail work and fine cutting. Small sharp scissors work best.

If you need an invitation or card for a special occasion, you can develop your own designs to add a personal touch to the event.

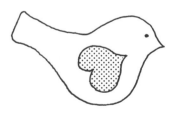

For a gift, package your "Country-Style" stationery in a zip-top bag, a coordinating tote bag you've made, or a box you've covered with calico to match the stationery. Please someone on your gift list with stationery you've trimmed.

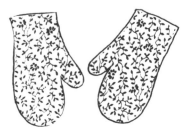

Alternating hearts make a pleasing border design.

Country Critters

Stitch a length of yarn extending from this ball. This cat's been busy!

goat

Eyes can be added to appliqués with French knots, fabric paint, machine stitching, or very tiny buttons.

Dashed lines indicate stitching lines.

These geese are framed in the photo on page 2. They were stitched onto "hopscotch" cross stitch fabric.

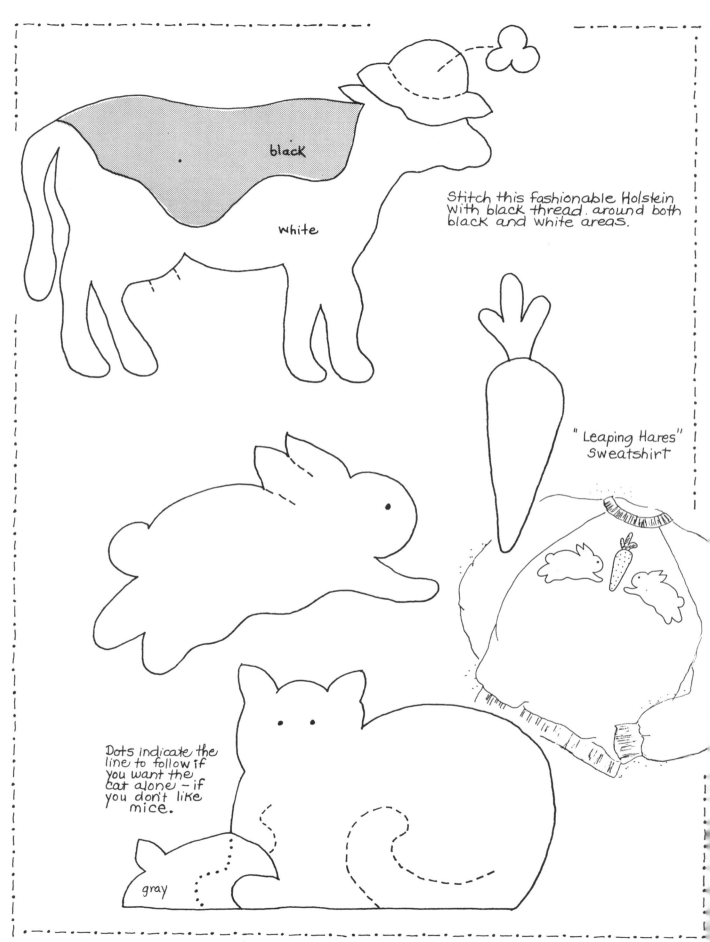

black

white

Stitch this fashionable Holstein with black thread. around both black and white areas.

"Leaping Hares" Sweatshirt

Dots indicate the line to follow if you want the cat alone — if you don't like mice.

gray

32

Find this design appliqued on a child's sweatshirt on page 1. Large buttons are used for the wagon wheels

P.S. If you like to do charted needlework, these applique designs offer many new possibilities.

Pig in a Poke

Combine the heart and two geese to create this pleasing, symmetrical design. Add ribbon bows to the necks for extra detail.

Celebrations and Occasions

Birthday cake

4th of July

white
blue
red
White
red
white

Easter

green
brown
orange

Halloween

white
orange
yellow

Candy corn

"Sprinkle" a few of these across the top of a butcher apron for a candy lover.

Appliqued Necklaces

For something different, stitch applique designs onto clothing to imitate a necklace. (See the spool necklace on page 1.)

Begin planning your necklace by trying on the garment and also a beaded necklace. Use pins or a washable marking pen to mark the curve of the necklace onto the garment.

Purchase 1½ yards of ⅛" wide ribbon for the "string" of the necklace. (I prefer grosgrain ribbon since it stays tied better.) Fuse Wonder-Under™ or Stitch Witchery to the back of 8" of ribbon,

Cut from fabric and lay out the design shapes along the necklace curve on the garment. Cut small pieces of the 8" section of ribbon to join the shapes in the curve. Slip the ends of the short ribbon pieces under the appliques.

Cut 2 longer pieces of ribbon at least 12" long to extend beyond the top applique shapes and tie behind the neck. Of course you can applique shapes all around the shirt's neckline if you prefer.

Fuse the applique shapes and small ribbon pieces to the garment. Don't forget to insert one end of each longer ribbon piece beneath the top applique shape. Applique stitching will hold the tie in place. Go ahead and sew.

With this "fake" necklace, you'll never have to worry about having the right piece of jewelry.

Bead Shapes

gingerbread people

Dashed lines indicate stitching lines.

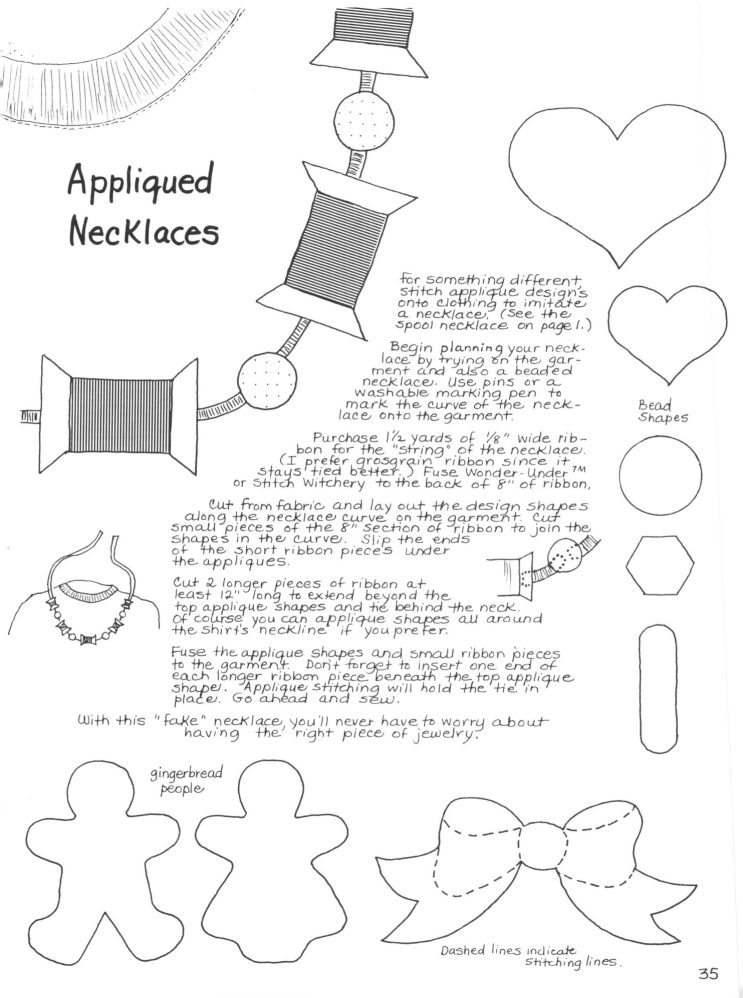

Teddy Bears

←small buttons sewed on add the detail of a jointed teddy bear.

Bearing my love to you...

optional headwear for See-Saw Teddy

optional scarf for See-Saw Teddy

The 3 Bears

Appliqued Album Cover

An appliqued book cover for a photo album protects the album, presents a design on an otherwise plain book, and is removable for laundering. Let's make one — it's easy and fun.

This is an album of sewing and stitchery projects I've completed. I hope you've started a photo collection of your works of art.

There may be other books you'd like to cover with fabric. Some possibilities:

- baby albums
- bird watching guides
- paperback books with "racy" titles

With the directions included here, you can construct covers for books of any size. We'll need a tape measure to begin this project...

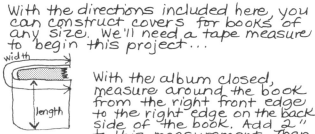

width

length

With the album closed, measure around the book from the right front edge to the right edge on the back side of the book. Add 2" to this measurement. Then measure the length of the book and add 1½" to the measurement.

Cut one piece of fabric to these 2 measurements. I prefer a quilted fabric (solid color), corduroy, or other heavier weight fabrics. Also cut 2 strips to the length measurement and 4" wide. (make them narrower if the book is small.) Add applique now.

width + 2"

length + ½"

4" 4"

length + 1½"

wrong side of strip

Turn under and stitch one long edge of each of the 4" strips.

right side of album cover

wrong side of fabric

Place the 2 strips with right sides down and seamed edge toward the center as indicated on the diagram. Pin in place and stitch around the 3 sides of each strip, using a ½" seam allowance.

Trim seam allowances and clip corners. Turn the cover right side out and try it on the album to make sure it fits.

raw edges

Turn back the remaining raw edges on the top and bottom of the album cover. Overcast or serge the edges or cover them with bias tape. Press toward inside of cover and hand stitch these edges in place to maintain a neat look to the album cover.

And now you're done.

Covered and decorated photo albums make great gifts.

Options to consider:

Add a shoulder strap to the cover for a bird book so the book can be carried conveniently on birding trips.

Attach a ribbon to the top center of the cover if you'd like to have a permanent book marker.

Ultrasuede® Checkbook Cover

What could be more elegant than a monogrammed Ultrasuede® checkbook cover with a pen holder?

With the directions below, you can make your own cover for a personal checkbook.

Ultrasuede® pieces to cut:

1 piece 6¾" x 6½" – piece A
2 pieces 3" x 6½" – pieces B
1 piece 2¼" x 2¼" – piece C
1 piece Velcro 1½" x ½"

Cut these pieces carefully with scissors or a rotary cutter. All edges must be smooth because they will show.

Begin by adding the monogram or applique to the front side of piece A.

Stitch one of the Velcro pieces to the center bottom of piece A, about ½" from the bottom edge. Sew the other section of Velcro to piece C near one edge.

With the right side of piece A down, place piece C (right side up) over the front edge of piece A. There is enough room to adjust this piece which will hold the pen. Plan to leave about 1½" extended past the edge of piece A to wrap around an average pen.

Place the B pieces, right side up, over the ends of piece A. Pin in place

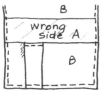

Stitch around the cover, using a ⅛" seam allowance. You may prefer to stitch from the top side of the cover. If you have trouble with skipped stitches, use a stretch needle on your machine.

If your checks need to be inserted in the cover on the left side, cut another piece of Ultrasuede® 1"x Stitch this to the left side of piece B to hold the checks in place.

Add thin cardboard inside the "pockets" formed by the B pieces if you would like a stiffer checkbook cover.

Just think – you'll no longer need to search for a pen when it's time to write a check.

abcdefghi
jklmnopqr
stuvwxyz

heart shape to use with monogram

ABCDEFG
HIJKLMN
OPQRST
UVWXYZ

Numbers 1, 2, 3 are found on page 9

456789

HOWDY

Just for fun, make a
little different kind of
"Welcome" sign.

The Page for Plans and Dreams
Country Projects I'd like to make:

Ideas I've used from this book

my magic needle

Instructions Index

Design Index

Readers,

By the time you reach this page, I hope you're inspired to try some of the designs and ideas in this book. Now that I've prepared all these pages, I'm ready to relax with some "fun" sewing projects. I plan to sew the wheat design at the bottom of this page.

The designs in this book can be adapted for other uses, just as this wheat design was adapted from a stencil. I am always interested to know how you have used my designs and I welcome your ideas, comments, and suggestions.

Mary

Other titles by Mary Mulari are available through fabric shops, notions catalogs or Mary's Productions. For information and brochures, please send self-addressed stamped legal size envelope to:

Titles available:

Designer Sweatshirts
Applique Design Collection
MORE Designer Sweatshirts
Country Style Appliques
Minnesota Appliques - folder

Mary's Productions
Box 87 - Dept. B4
Aurora, Minnesota 55705

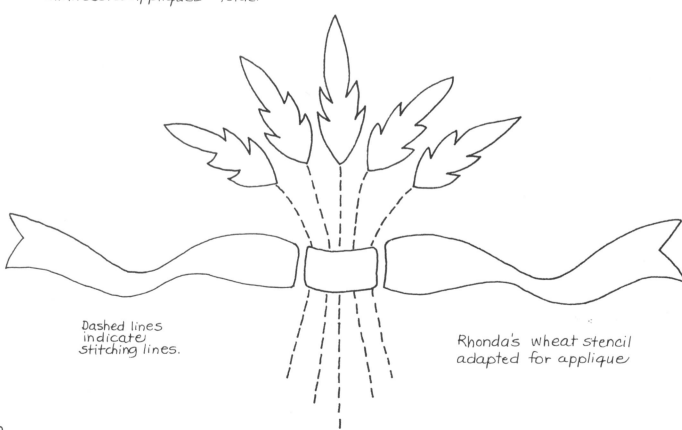

Dashed lines indicate stitching lines.

Rhonda's wheat stencil adapted for applique